FEDERICO FEDERICI

LINER NOTES FOR A PITHECANTHROPUS ERECTUS SKETCHBOOK

a pure asemic tribute to Charles Mingus

with a solo by

SJ Fowler

LN

libri della neve

Cover: *Pithecanthropus Erectus*, Federico Federici 2018
Private Collection

http://federicofederici.net
http://www.stevenjfowler.com/
http://leserpent.wordpress.com

libri della neve
PRINTED ON EARTH

SJ Fowler

uno

And after three days of writing listening, Federico just had an
inkling to go on home. So he walked down Coldharbour Lane,
head hung low; three or four in the morning; the sun was coming
up and the birds were out singing. He let himself into a pad. He
wound his way up a spiral staircase and stretched himself out nice-
ly on the chesterfield. *Pithecanthropus Erectus* was already on the CD
player and he pushed that remote button to sublimity. He listened
to the sculptural rhythms of Charles Mingus. And J.R. Monterose
and Jackie McLean dueted unknown on saxophones and the sound
made its way out of the window, mingling with the traffic noises
outside and all of a sudden he was overcome by a feeling of brief
mortality. Mortality that was not lengthy, or durable, but explicitly
brief. Curtailed. Because he was getting on in the world. Coming
up on more years. More stony grey steps towards the grave. The
box. And just like Charles Mingus wrote *Epitaph* for Eric Dolphy,
Federico said to himself «so long Eric, so long John Coltrane and
Charles Mingus, so long Duke Ellington and Lester Young, so long
Billie Holiday and Ella Fitzgerald, so long Jimmy Reed, so long
Muddy Waters, and so long Howling Wolf.»

due

Pithecanthropus erectus redirects here. For the song and album
by that title, see *Pithecanthropus Erectus* (album). The fossil aroused
much controversy. Less than ten years after 1891, almost eighty
books or articles had been published on Dubois's finds. Despite
Dubois's argument, few accepted that Java Man was a transitional
form between apes and humans. Some dismissed the fossils as apes
and others as modern humans, whereas many scientists considered

Java Man as a primitive side branch of evolution not related to modern humans at all. In the 1930s Dubois made the claim that Pithecanthropus was built like a "giant gibbon", a much misinterpreted attempt by Dubois to prove that it was the "missing link".

tre

My feeling on the poems is that they are a cohesive set, yet each has its own identity. How much time the reader spends with each is up to them, but they might spend hours, or seconds, with each or with all. How rare is a clear control of the pansemic aesthetic? Essentially it seems as though Federico's poems are often the evocation of a structure evading itself, an exact match to what Mingus declared his piece was about – a ten minute tone poem. Certainly in terms of actual construction Federico is also providing a score, a rescoring of that which been unscored. Here is metaphorical language without semantics. Ambiguous detail activating the poetic. The work is remarkable precisely because it works in a graceful, familiar space to do often stark and unfamiliar things. Like jazz that absorbs sound. This feels to me a faithful act towards listening and the intention towards possibility and inspiration. The roll, the smudge, the dead signature. The cut in the scrawl. The squig. The line, cards and bled ink. Sounds on paper.

F Federici

This collection of sheets is a purely asemic tone poem, sketching the mood of the first man to stand erect, taking inspiration from the musically depicted portrait given by Charles Mingus, in his *Pithecanthropus Erectus*.

Aiming at dealing with the story of mankind in its own way, asemic writing seemed the most appropriate choice, insisting upon semiotics, rather than idioms.

Overcome with his alleged superiority over the trees, likewise standing erect, but unmoving in the background, and over the animals, still in a prone position, man first conceived of conquering the Earth, then of eventually ruling Nature. Given these assumptions, his sought emancipation led to solitude and self-enslaving.

As the original jazz suite, this poem can be loosely divided into four movements:

> *evolution*, p. 9–21
> *superiority-complex*, p. 22–45
> *decline*, p. 46–51
> *destruction*, p. 53–56

The first movement sets the elementary shapes (dots, stains, lines), which get later on, in the second movement especially, organized into more complex dynamic structures or repeated solos.

The introduction to the third movement, instead, registers a much more organic disturbance in the whole pattern. Further attempts to regain control over that first frantic signs of crisis fail.

The fourth movement is again based on the third, except that it develops into an increasing complexity ending with blank language lines, resembling those on page 28 and 29, but somehow unnaturally upwards, no longer organized into blocks.

The final, definite climax is a white fallout, an unexpressed ultimate (or even anew primordial) act.

London, Coldharbour Lane

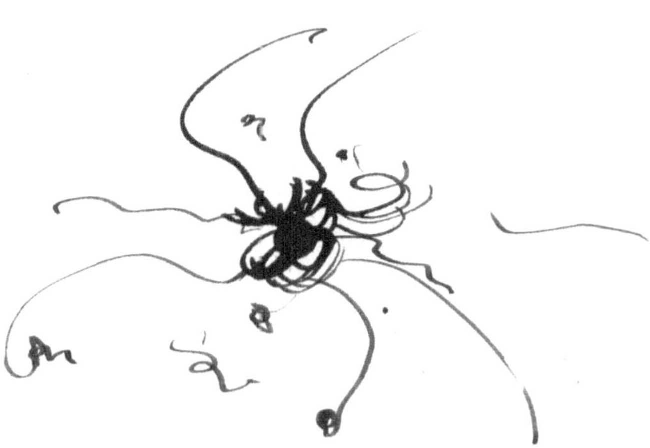

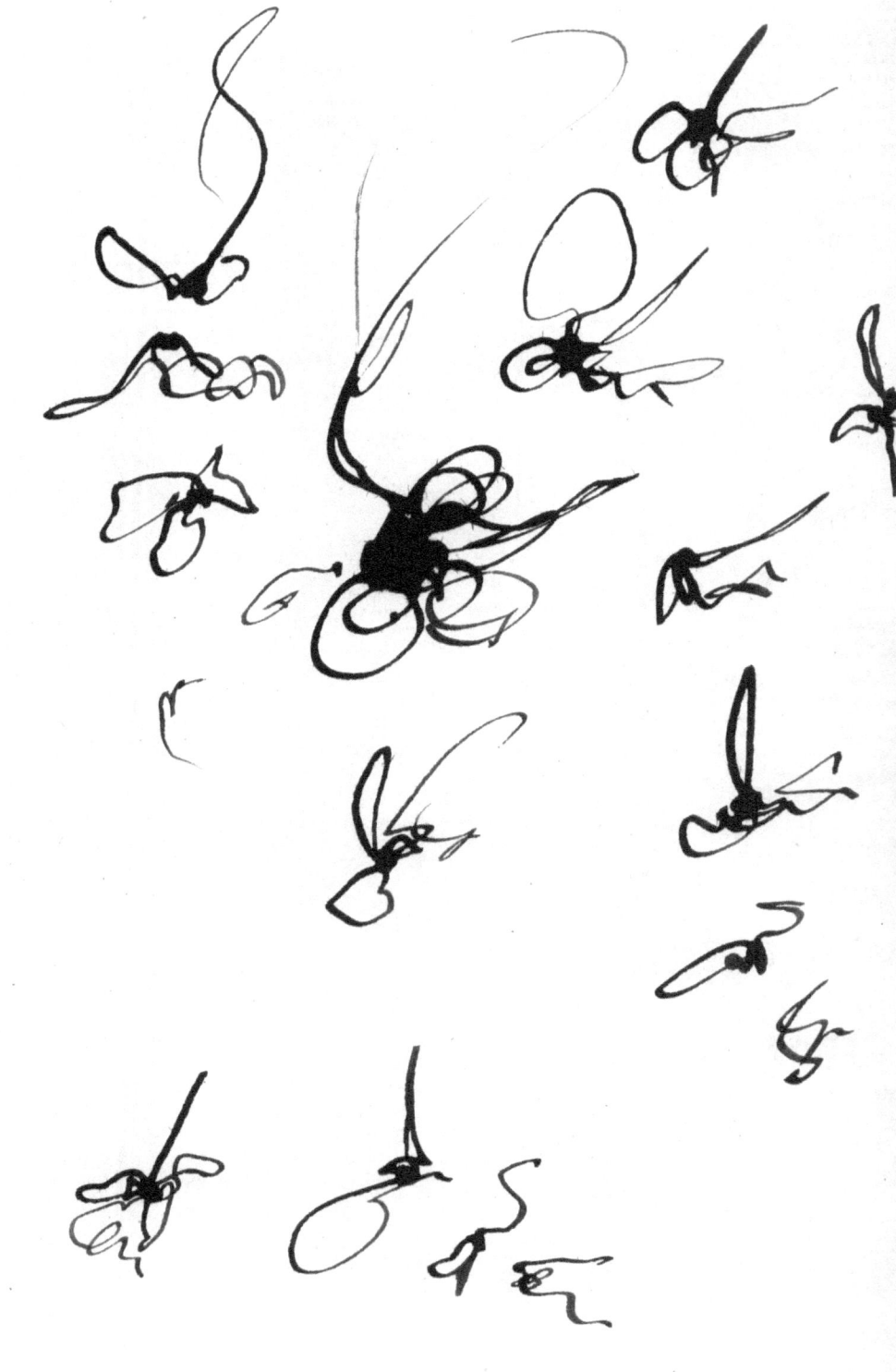

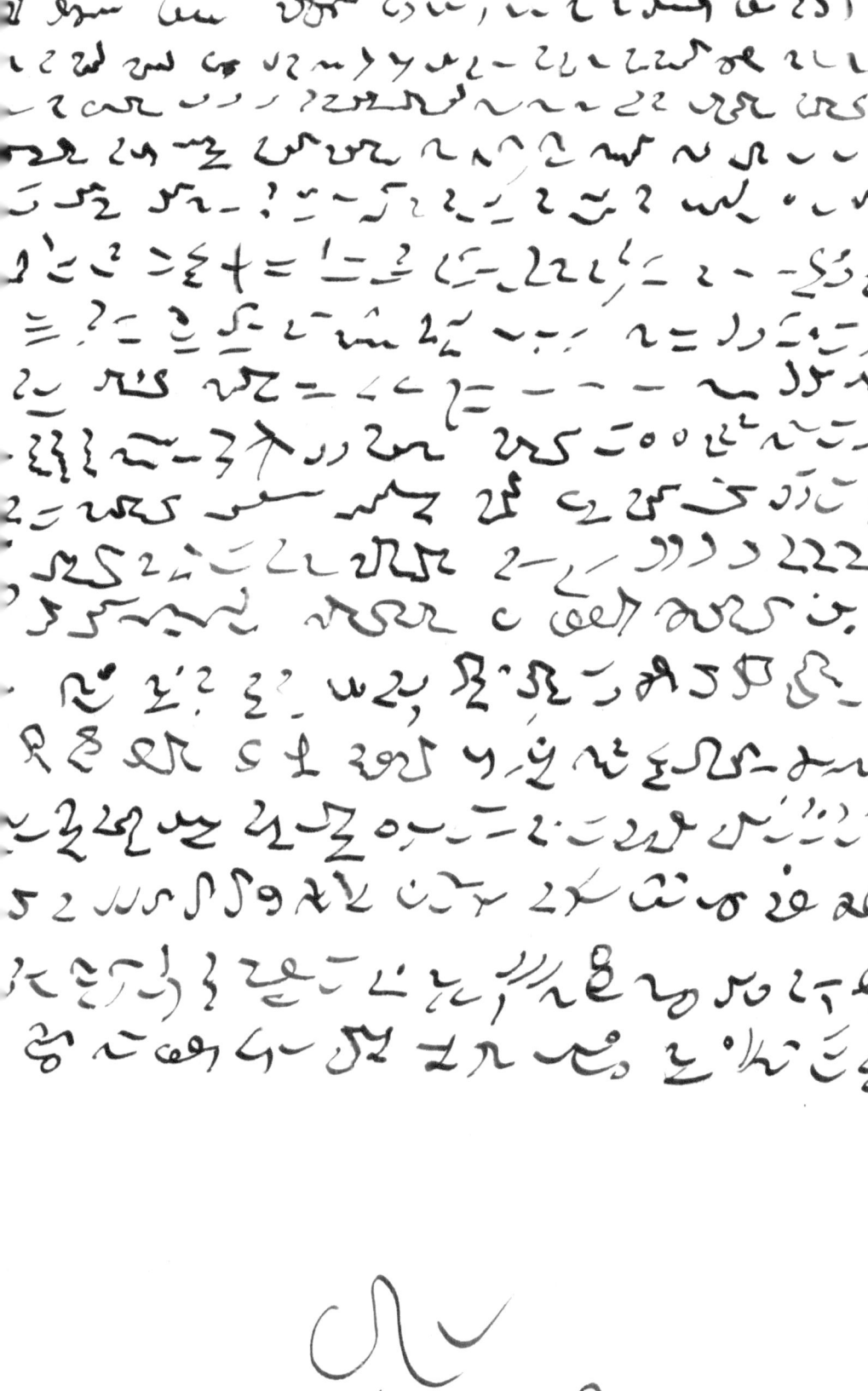

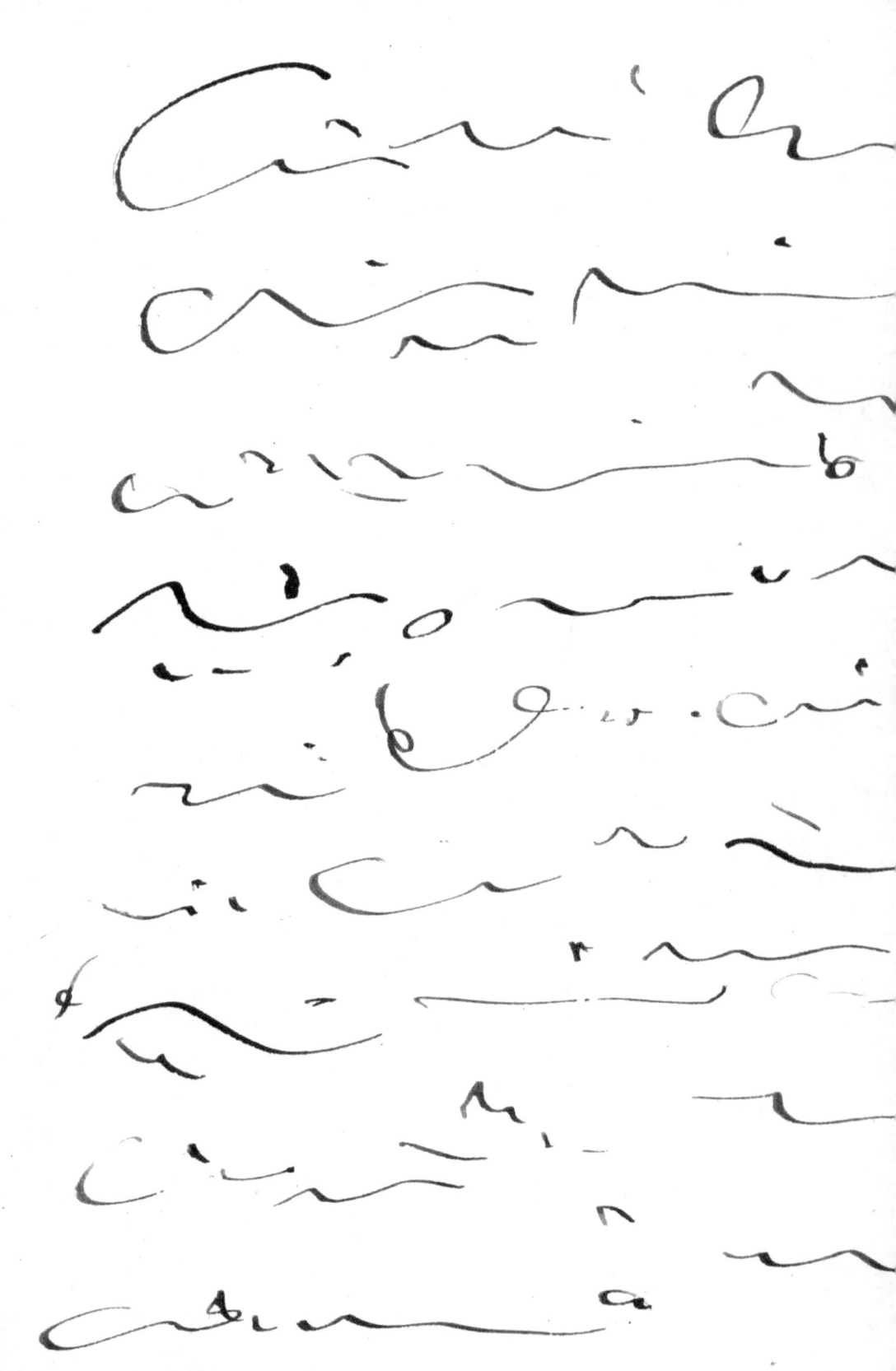

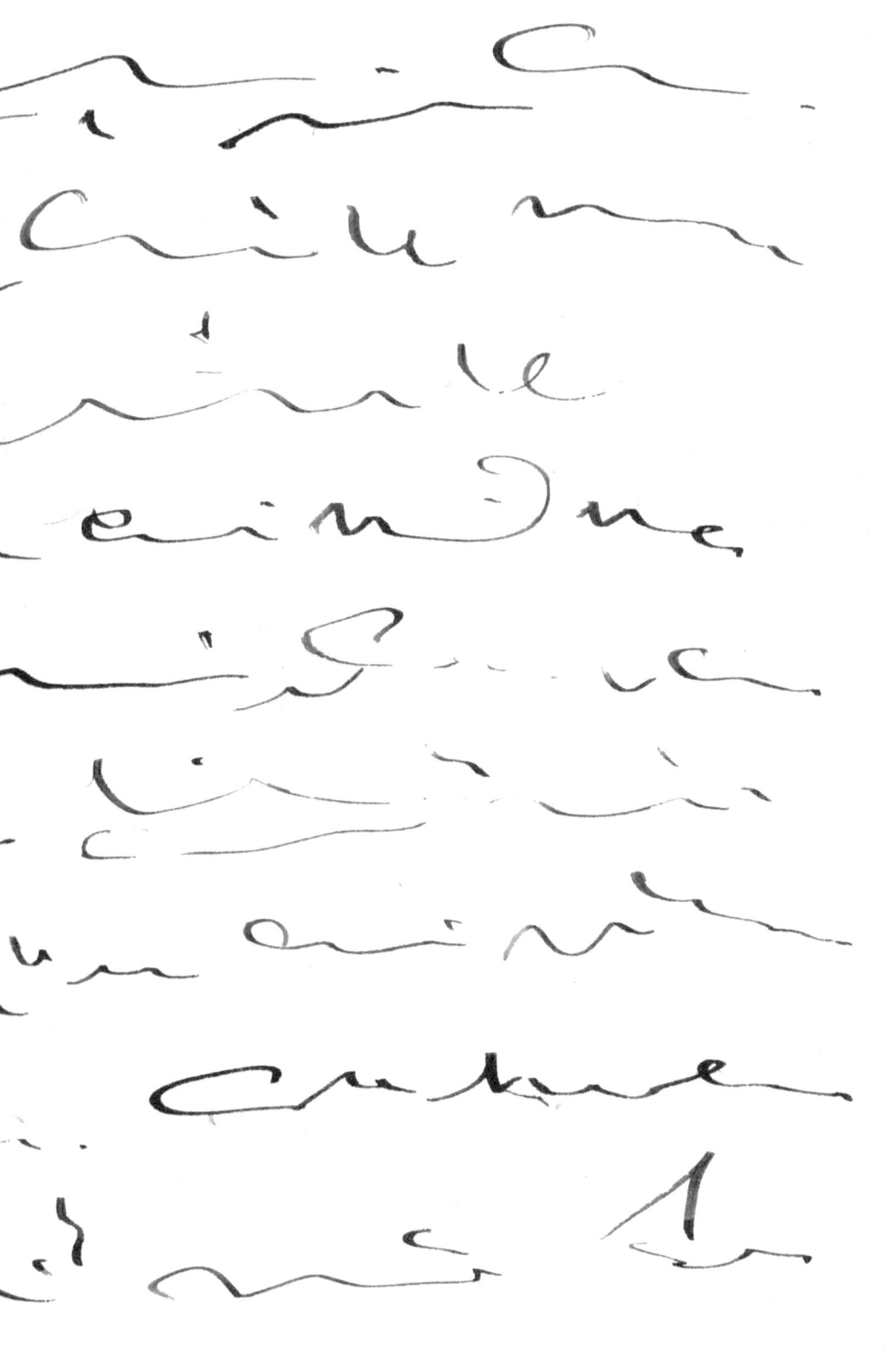

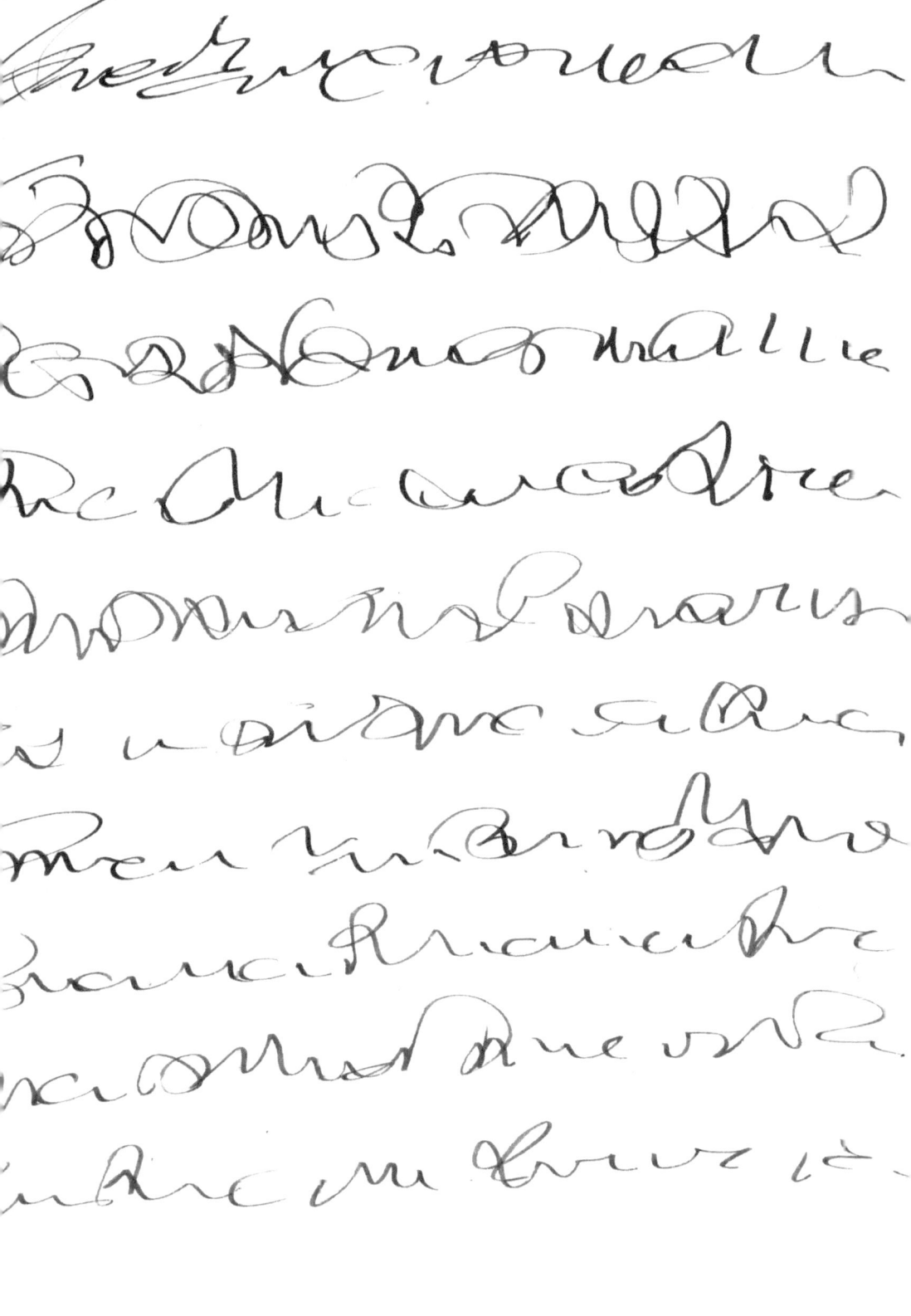

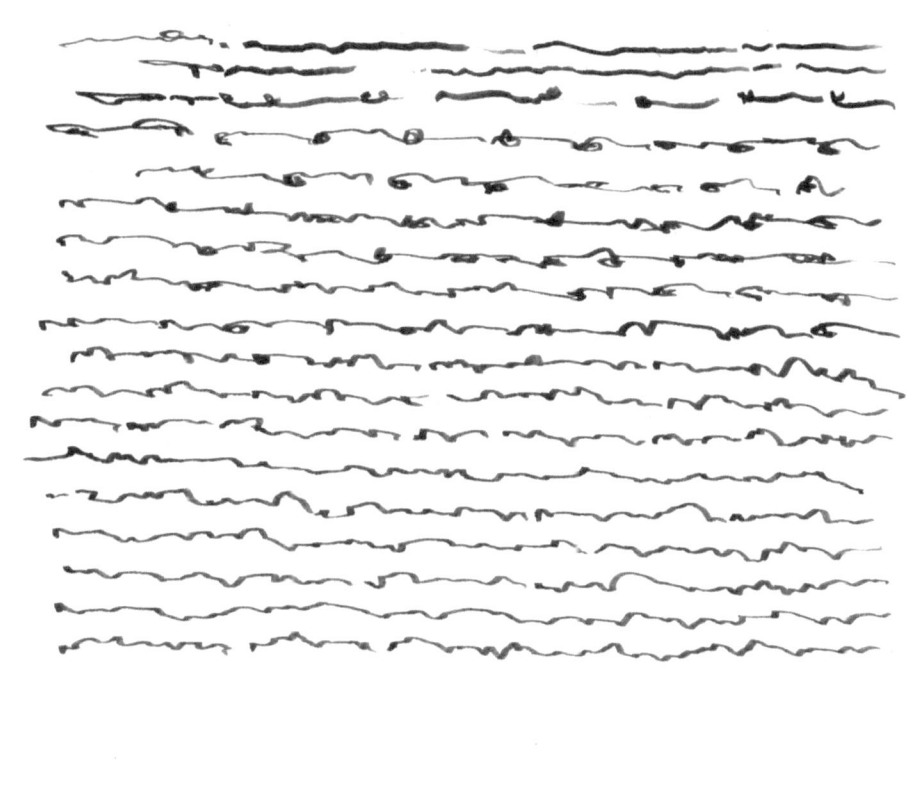

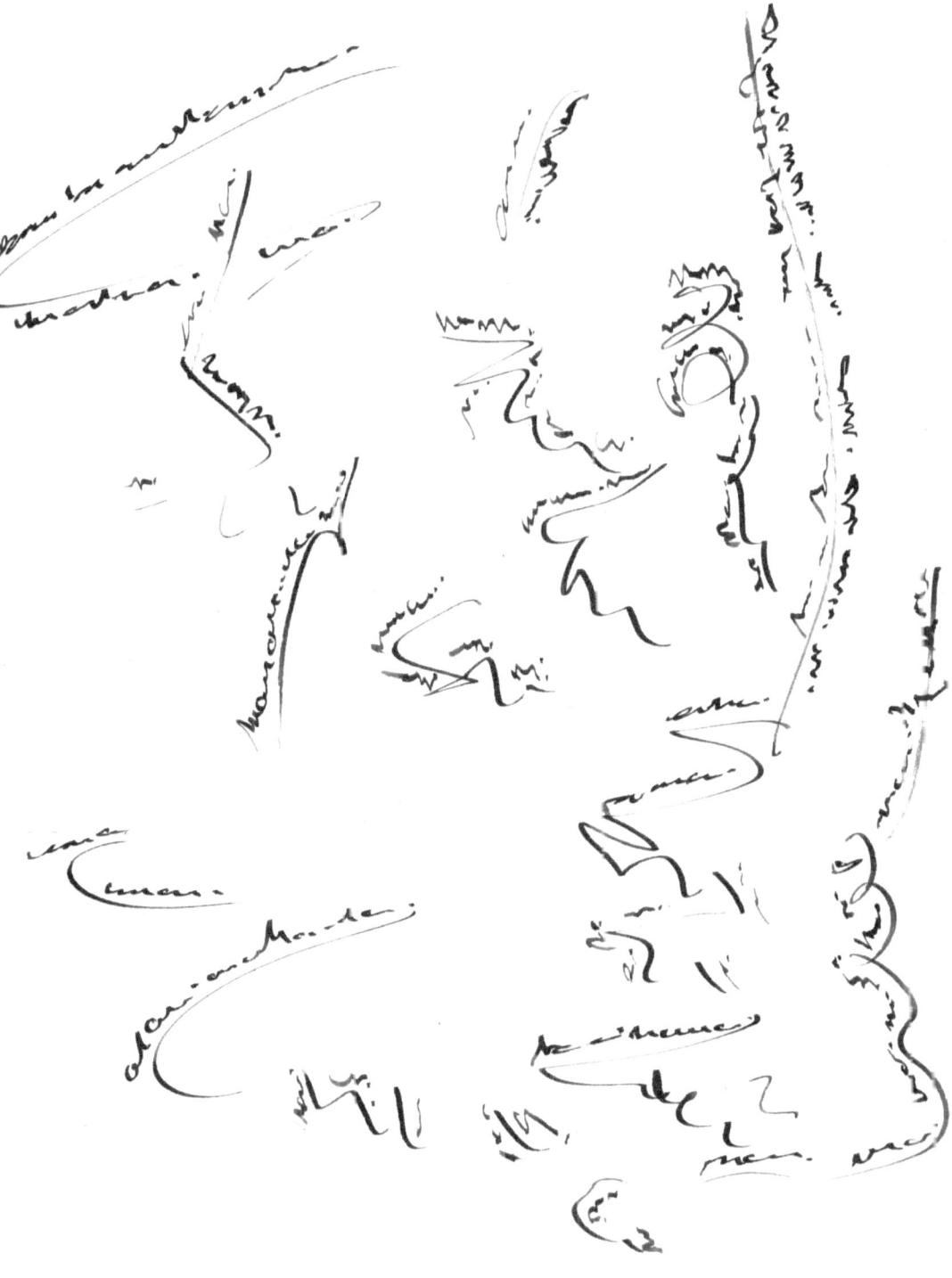

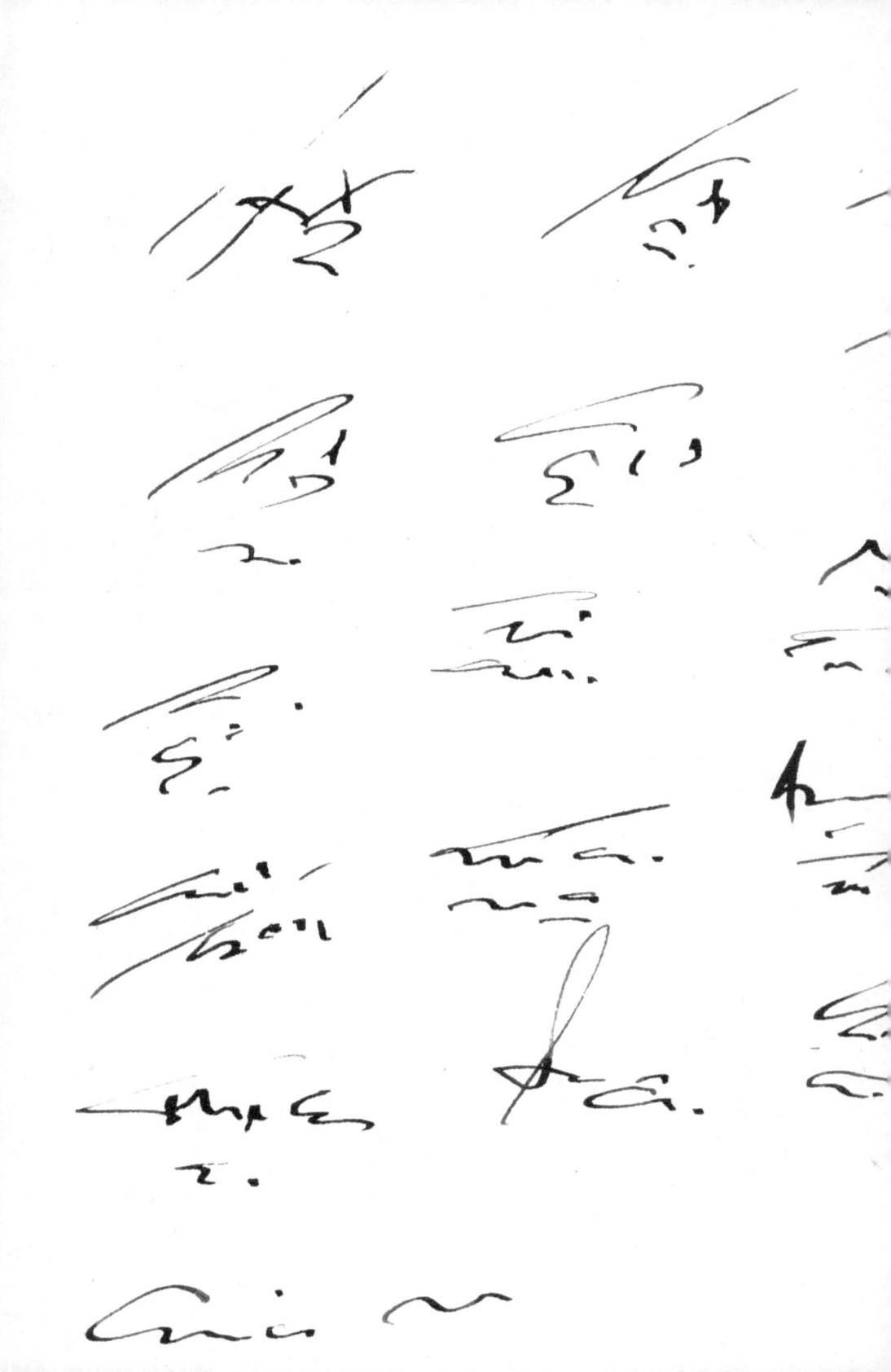

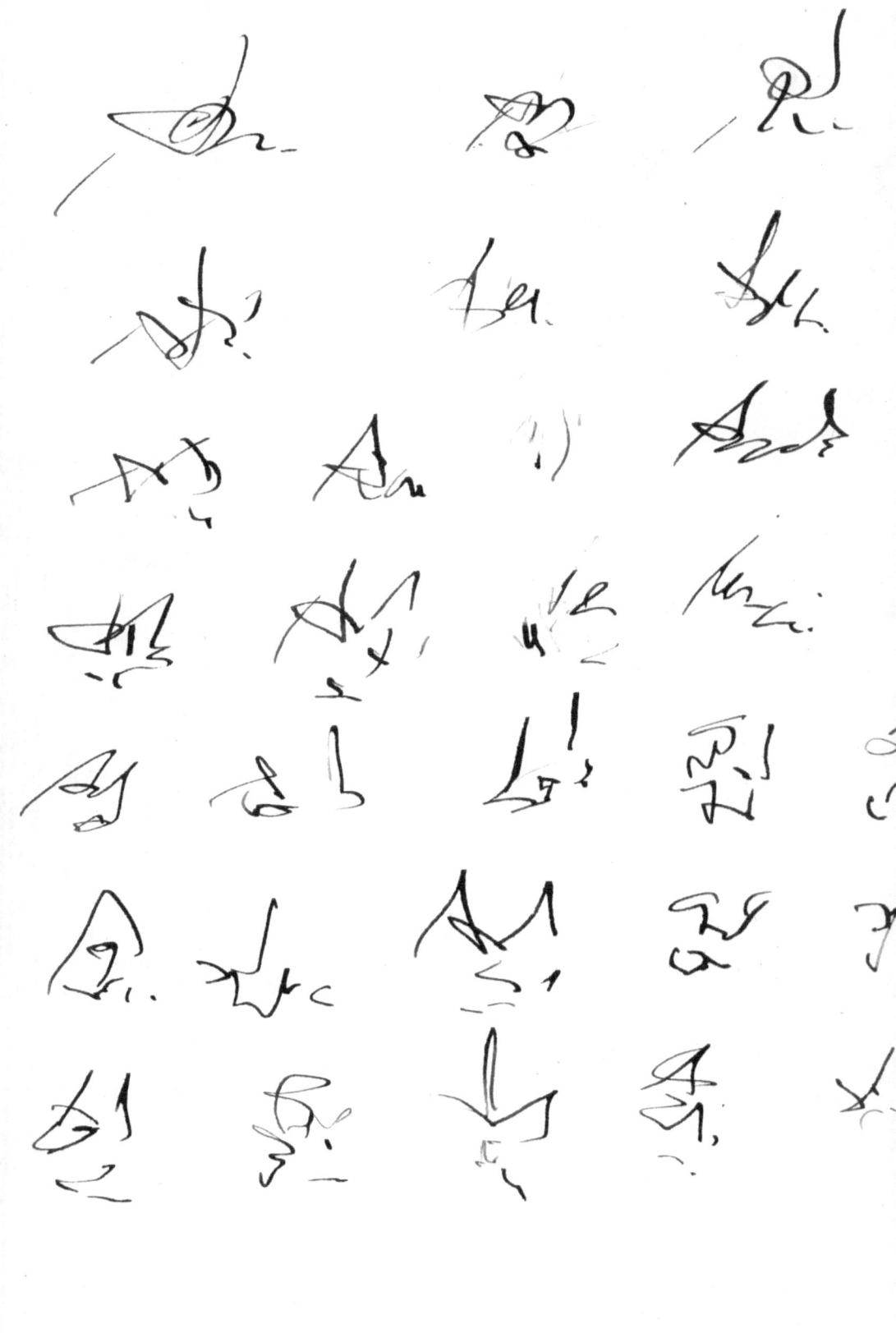

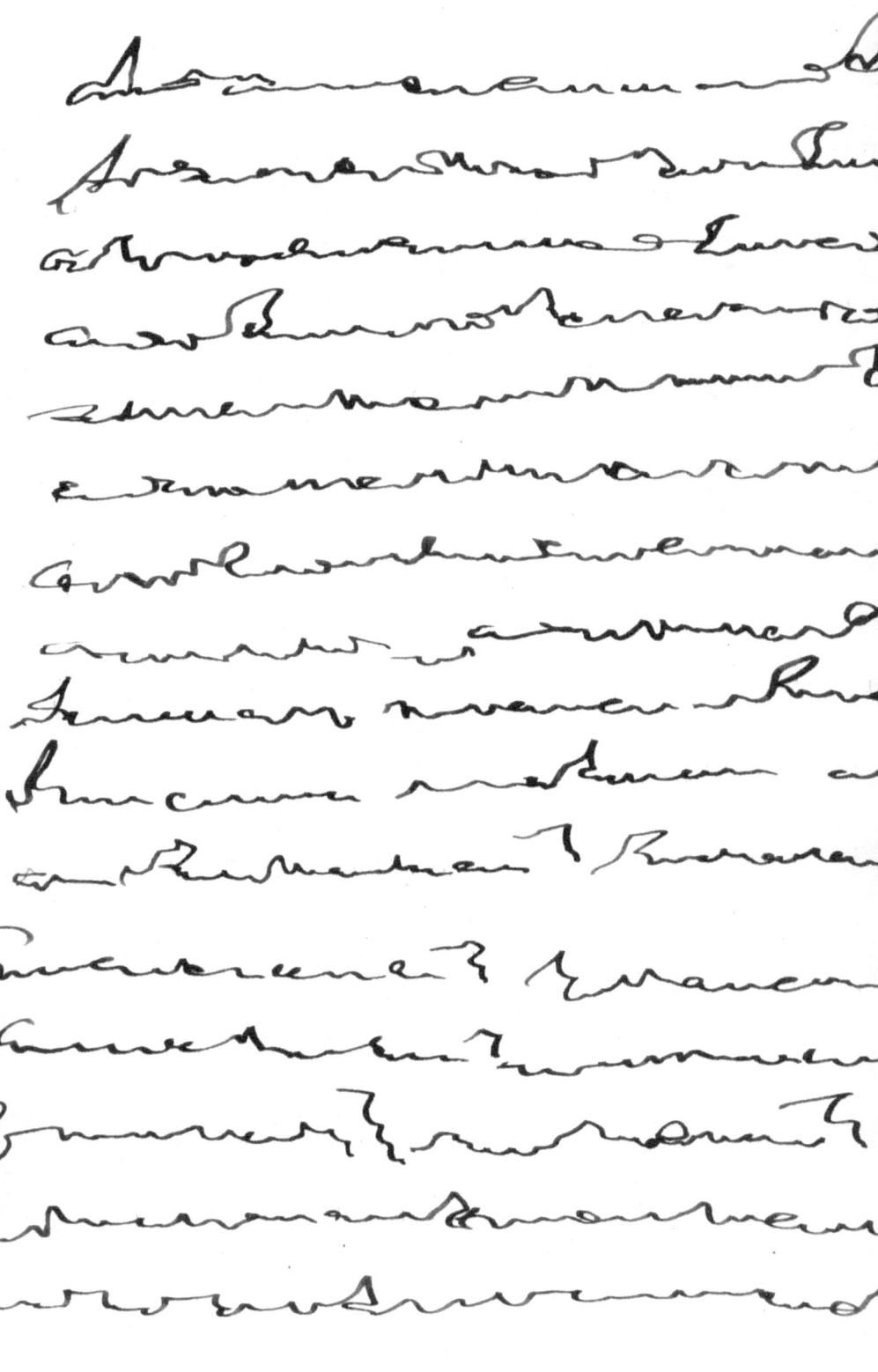

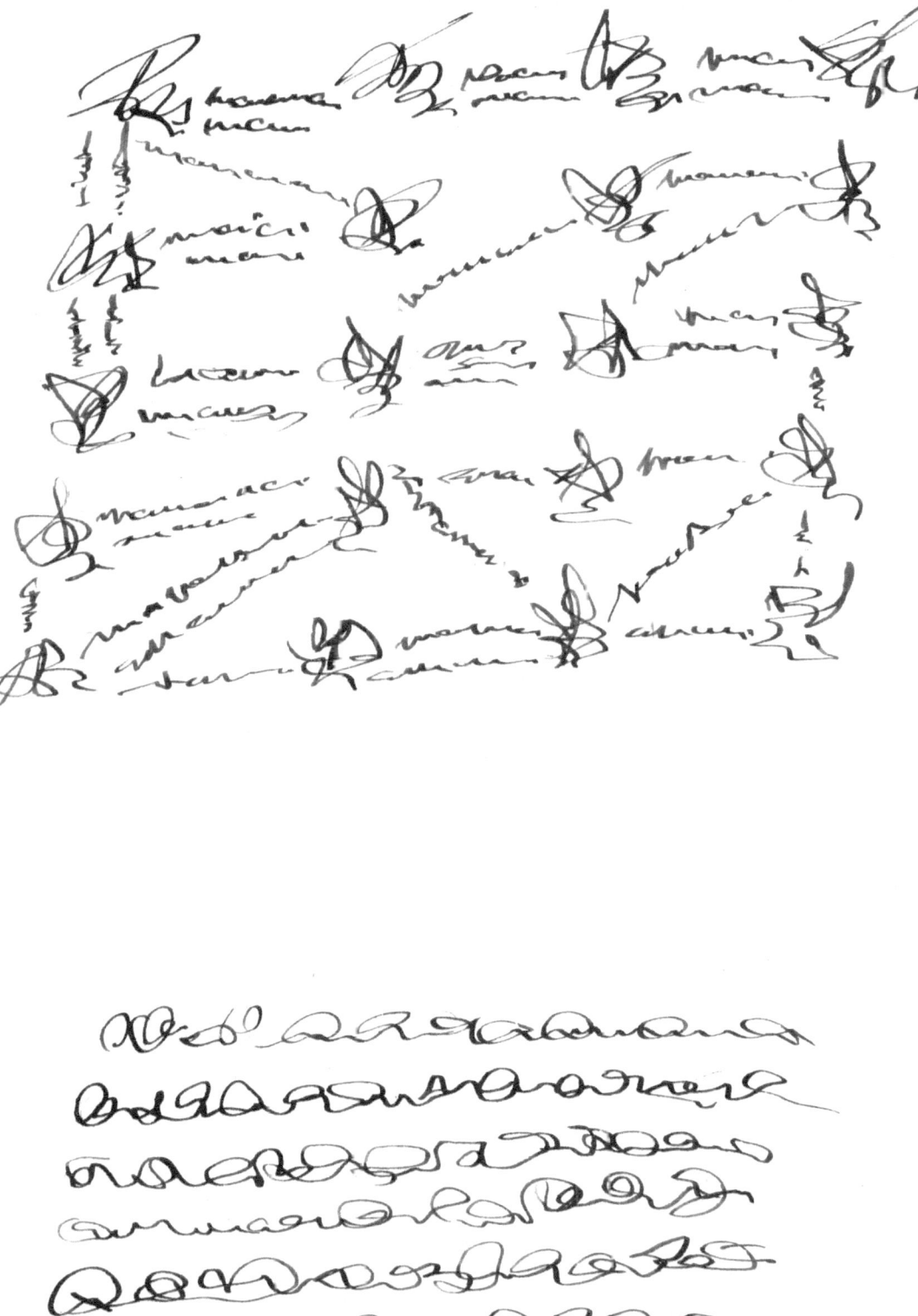

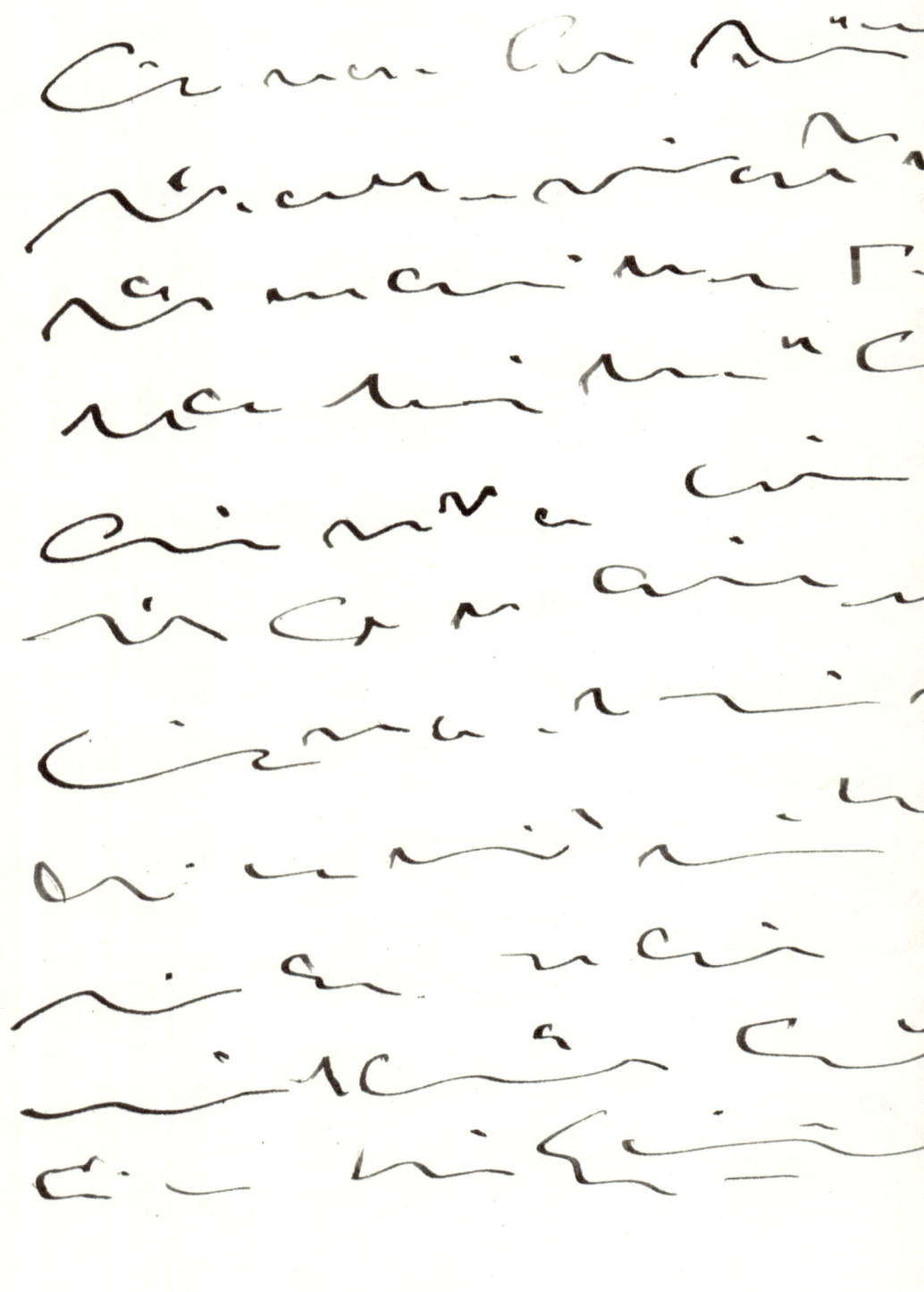

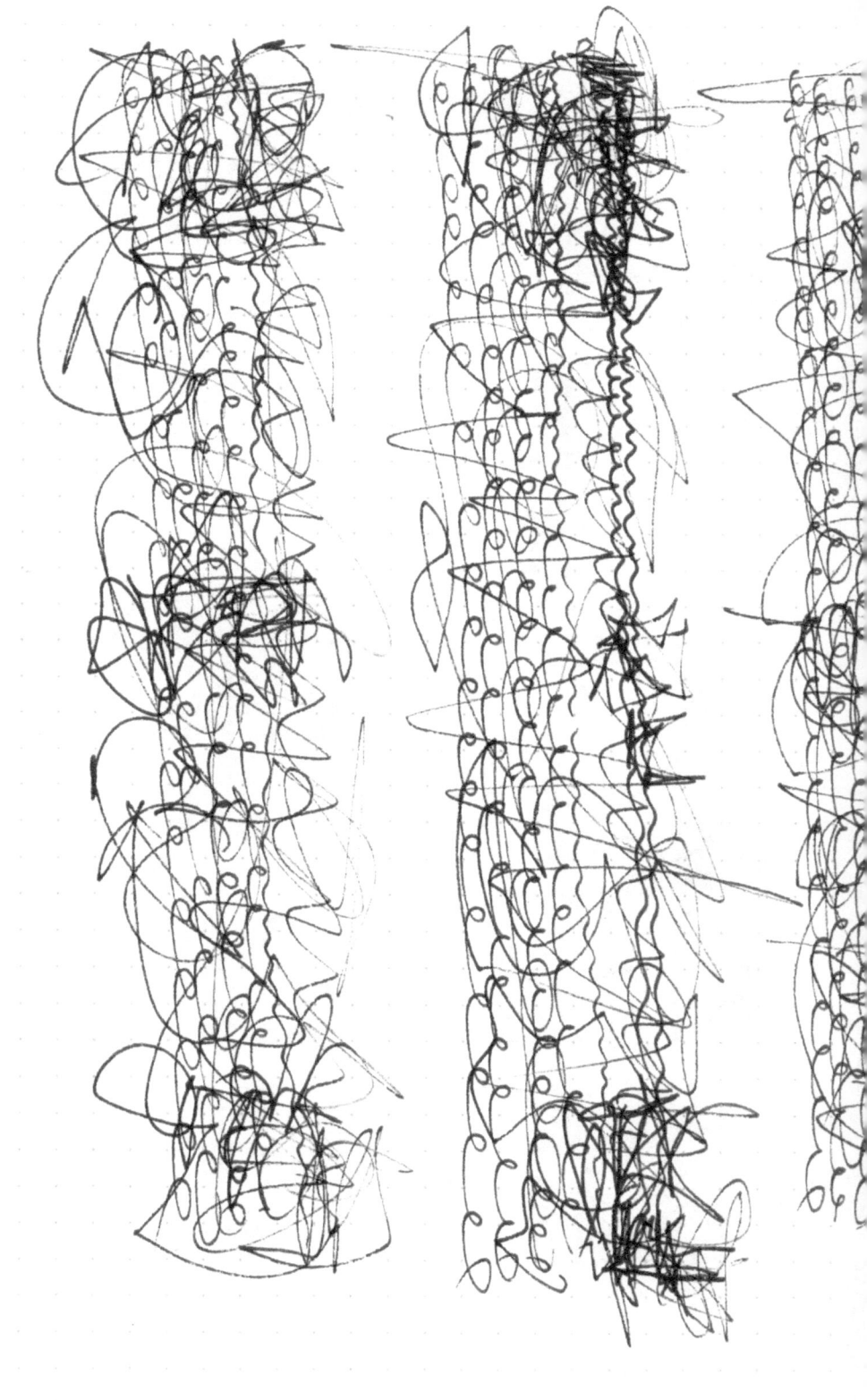

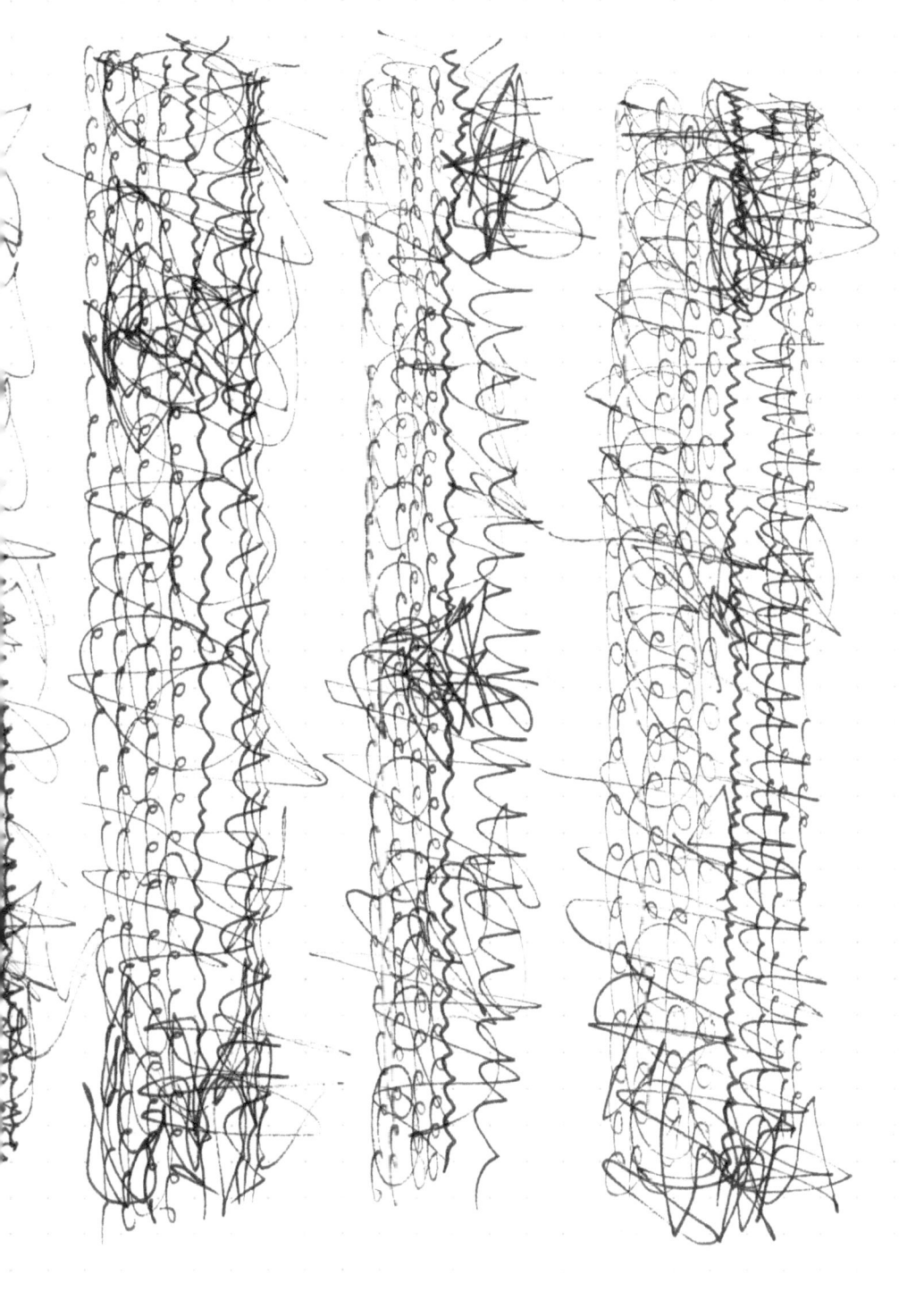

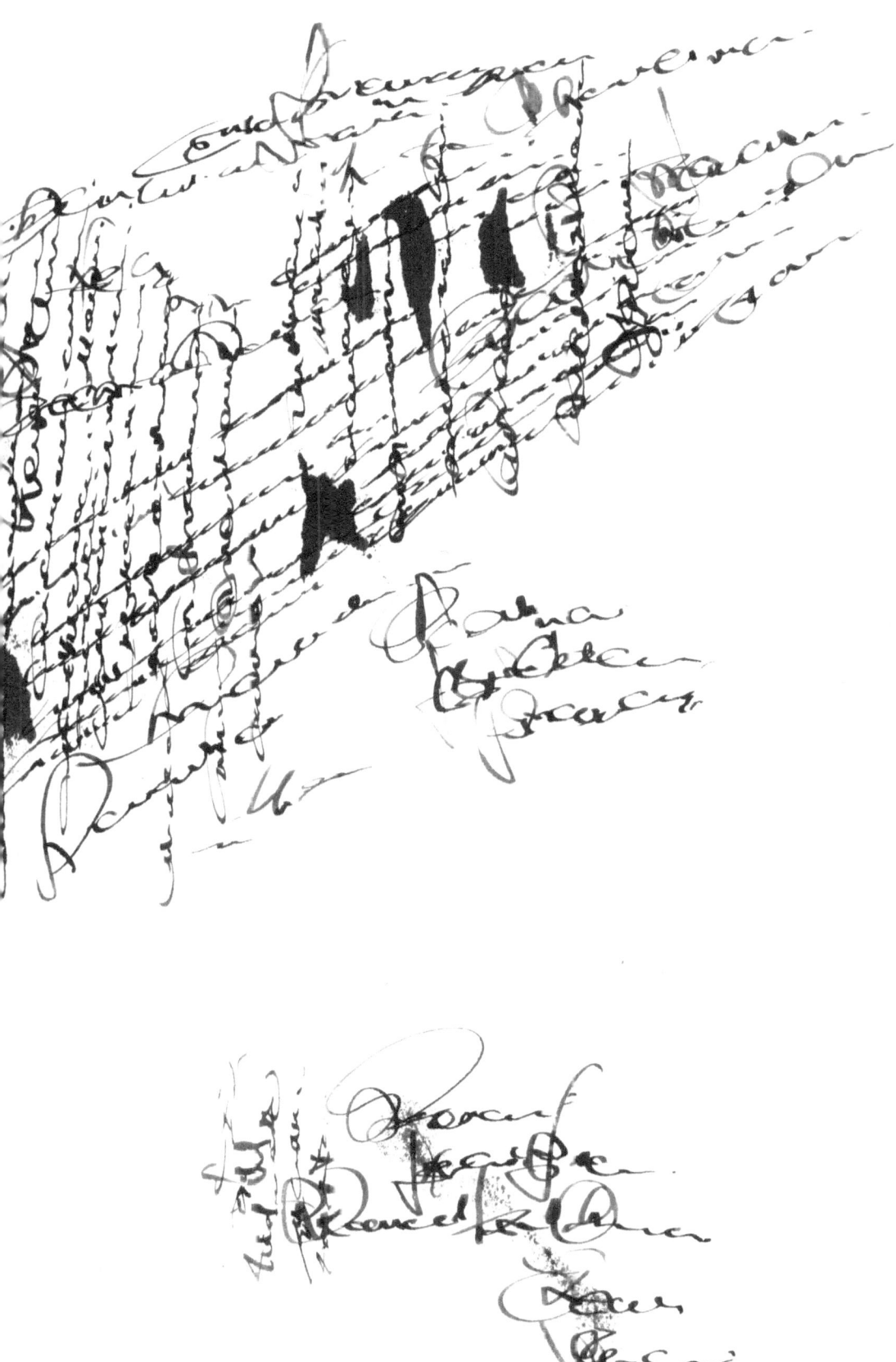

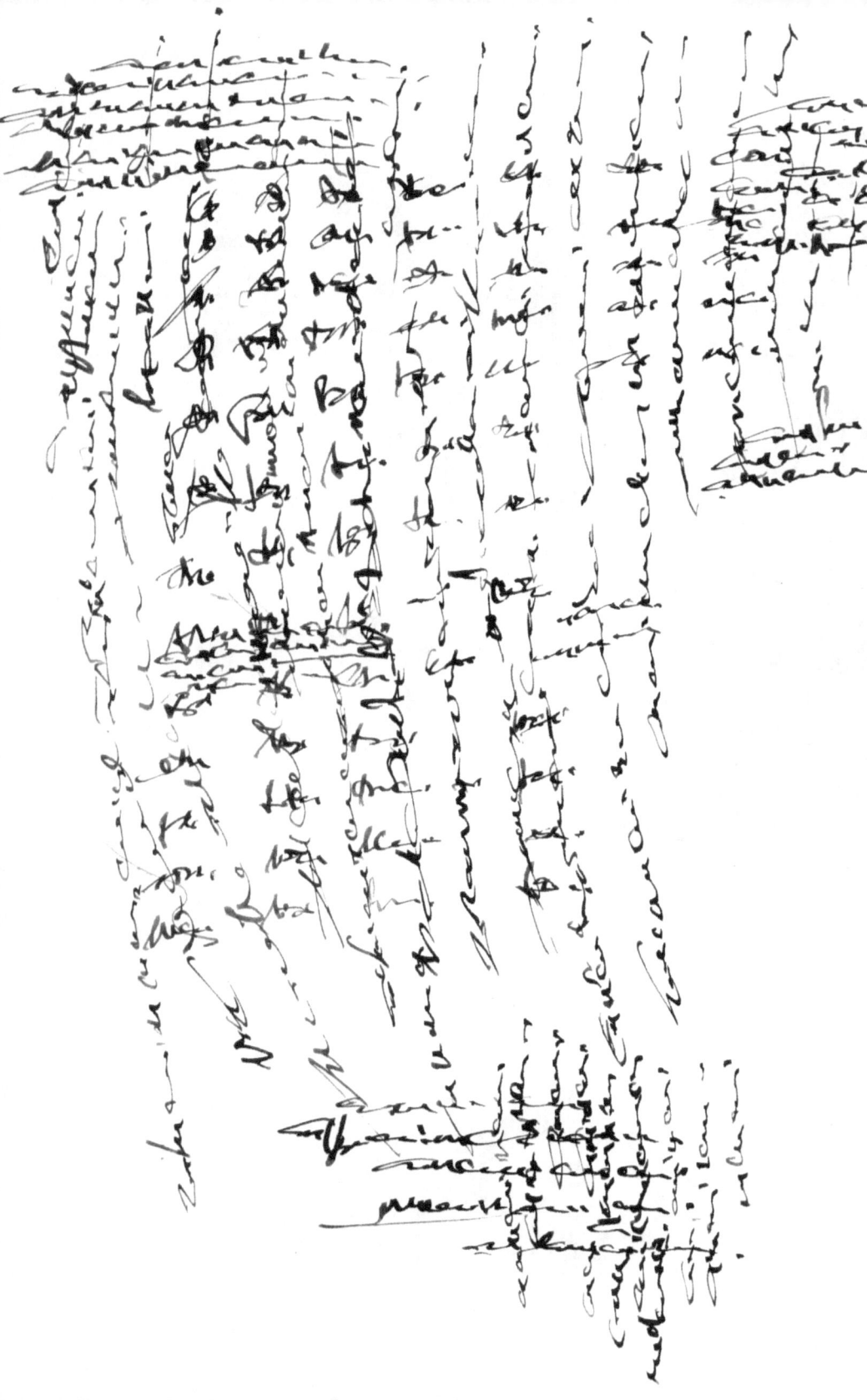

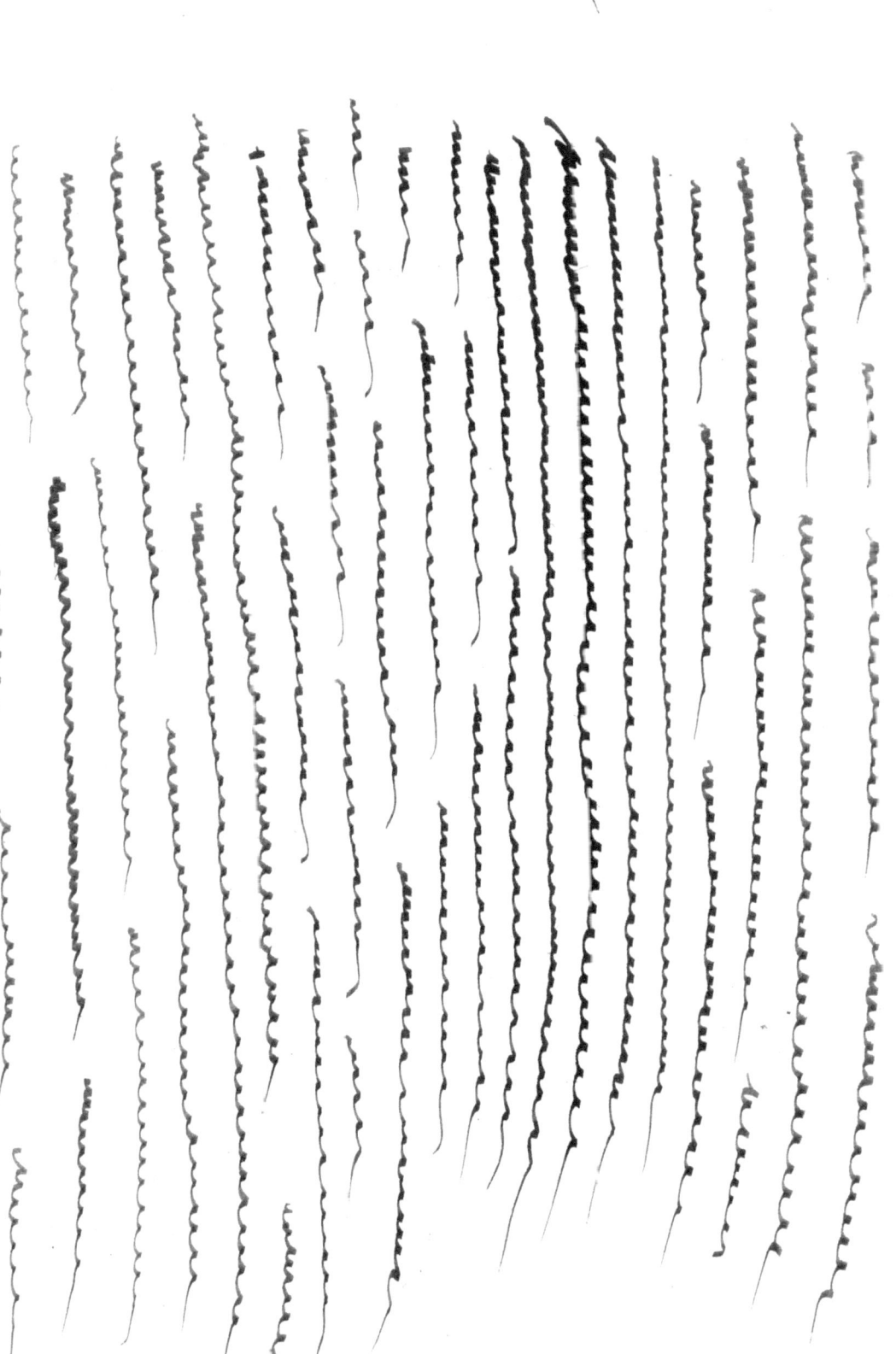

This page was intentionally left blank.